I0200892

A Jewish Athlete

Swimming Against Stereotype
in 20th Century Europe

A Jewish Athlete

Swimming Against Stereotype
in 20th Century Europe

by Helen Epstein

PLUNKETT LAKE PRESS
Lexington, Massachusetts

© 2006 Helen Epstein

All rights reserved. Except for brief passages quoted in newspaper, magazine, online, radio or television reviews, no part of this book may be reproduced in any form or by any means, electronic or mechanical, including photocopying or recording, or by any information storage or retrieval system, without permission in writing from the Publisher.

ISBN: 978-0-9614696-7-2

First Plunkett Lake Press paperback edition, 2019

plunkettlakepress.com

Also available from Plunkett Lake Press as an electronic book: plunkettlakepress.com/aja

For Kurt Epstein's grandchildren,
whom he never knew:
Daniel, Sam, Jessy, Max and Laura

Preface

My father Kurt Epstein was a tall, strong, active presence in our household and although I adored him, for most of my life I had no desire to investigate his career as an Olympic athlete. It was my artistic, depressive, intellectual mother who occupied center stage in our household. Kurt Epstein, born in the sleepy town of Roudnice-on-the-Elbe was cheerful, optimistic, and markedly less verbal than my mother. She spoke four languages fluently; my father was comfortable only in Czech. When I was a child, he took evening classes to learn English, and dutifully repeated simple homework assignments such as Benjamin Franklin's maxims, "Haste makes waste," and "Early to bed, early to rise, makes a man healthy, wealthy and wise" in a heavy accent. For much of my childhood, he read *Reader's Digest* condensed books.

He had been quite famous as a water polo player and swimmer during the first two decades of the Czechoslovak Republic. He became even more notorious when, in 1936, he defied Hitler and an international boycott of the Nazi Olympics and chose to participate in them, playing water polo for the Czechoslovak national team in Berlin. Five years later, he was deported to Terezín, the former Czechoslovak military garrison where he had been a reserve lieutenant and quartermaster. It had been designated as Ghetto Theresienstadt, one of Hitler's concentration camps. This time, he was again a quartermaster but also a Jewish prisoner. He survived there, briefly in Auschwitz, and in a forced labor camp, Kurt said, because he had been lucky and because he had been imprisoned with friends. After he returned to Prague in 1945, he became a member of the Czechoslovak National Olympic Committee and continued to coach swimming. His close friend and teammate, Pepik Bušek, had saved Kurt's sports scrapbook and returned it to him. It contained some of the articles and photographs reproduced in this book.

In February of 1948, during the Communist take-over of the country where his family had lived for four centuries, Kurt Epstein had decided to get out "in only a bathing suit if necessary." I often heard him say that the Communists were "Nazis in different color uniforms." Had he, his wife Franci, and baby daughter — me — remained in Prague, Kurt was sure that we would not have survived a second totalitarian regime.

So, in the summer of 1948, the three Epsteins moved into the Hotel Colonial opposite the Planetarium on 81st Street on the Upper West Side of Manhattan and three weeks later, my mother Franci began the dressmaking business that would support the family for a decade. Her first clients came from the Czech émigré community, referred by the famous Czech émigré physician Karel Steinbach. Kurt, who was then 44 years old, took a series of temporary jobs when and where he could find them.

Unfortunately for my father, water polo was all but unknown in New York City in 1948 and year-round swimming pools few and far between. Swimming was something people did at public beaches or private lakefronts in the summer or, maybe, at the YMCA if they were enthusiasts. My father often sat at home leafing through his scrapbook of sports photographs and clippings, among the very few possessions he had brought to New York from Czechoslovakia. He liked to share the scrapbook with me but as a young American girl, I had been embarrassed by them, both because, in the photos from the 1920s, men were still wearing women's bathing suits and, in some of the later snapshots, their briefs were so tight that their genitals were clearly outlined beneath the black cloth.

Today, when "working out" has become more common for many Americans than reading, it's impossible to convey how bizarre my father's old photo album and daily athletic discipline appeared in the 1950s. Every morning, he took a cold shower. Once every week, he took the subway to the Hotel St. George in Brooklyn where there was an Olympic-size pool, filled with 168,000 gallons of salt-water, with an enormous mirrored ceiling, and a waterfall at one end. He swam a couple of miles, and then had a massage. Sometimes he took me and my brother with him and we played beneath the waterfall while he did his laps.

ST. GEORGE
Natural · Salt · Water
SWIMMING · POOL

The Most Luxurious in the World.

Kurt taught my two brothers, Tommy and David, and me not only to swim, but to dive, ice skate, row, ride a bicycle, play tennis, ping-pong, basketball, soccer. He was a strict coach, but took as much pleasure in sports as other fathers took pleasure in their indoor artistic, intellectual, and professional work. Kurt preferred to teach us outside, in Central Park or Riverside Park, or in state parks outside the city such as Bear Mountain or Jones Beach. Every Saturday morning, he would wake us up at 7 AM and unless it was really foul weather, prod us into the car to drive out of the city to breathe fresh air. He recited Czech poetry about the sun, Latin maxims about health, and proverbs about competition such as "It's not whether you win or lose but how you play the game."

Tommy, Kurt and David in the mid 1960s.

He was an avid reader of the sports pages, and on occasion, treated himself and us to cheap tickets to basketball and ice hockey games — which I only now realize were, for him, substitutes for water polo. He liked to follow the careers of athletes of Czech origin such as basketball player John Havlicek. In the 1960s, he served as Treasurer of a Cold War outfit called The Association of Czechoslovak Sportsmen in Exile in the Western World. As a child and even as a teenager, I thought all of this was too weird to talk about. It's only now, when

I'm about the age Kurt was when he died, that I can see the extraordinary father he was.

My father died of a heart attack when he had just turned 71 and I was 27. We had more of an intuitive understanding between us than a verbal relationship. I used him as a jungle gym on land and as an anchor in the ocean. He taught me to defy fear, to dive off the high board and into cold water, and to develop persistence and a tolerance for frustration when I was learning something new. While I never became an amateur athlete, both my brothers and several of Kurt's grandchildren did.

The Cold War began and the Iron Curtain came down just after we emigrated, making it impossible for him to ever return to Czechoslovakia and difficult to correspond freely with his friends. Despite censors who inspected his letters, Kurt wrote regularly to friends in Czechoslovakia. In New York City, he spent a lot of time rehashing the political history of his country, trying to determine whether it could have been any different. His circle of refugee friends respected him as a champion athlete as a matter of course, in contrast to American anti-Semites such as the automobile magnate Henry Ford who declared: "Jews are not sportsmen."

Growing up in the United States, I realized that Ford was not alone in perpetuating that idea. Jewish athletes are often the subject of stereotypical jokes, sometimes told by Jews themselves. In the American film *Airplane*, for example, a stewardess asks a passenger whether she would like something to read.

"Do you have anything light?" asks the passenger.

"How about this leaflet: Jewish sports legends."

Growing up with a Jewish father who was an athlete to his core, I never understood the *Airplane* joke. At first, I was confused by it; then annoyed; then angry. I realized that, although for Hitler it had made no difference, elsewhere intellectual men such as Woody Allen or Philip Roth were widely regarded as "authentic" Jews while sports figures like Kurt Epstein were not. For a while after he died, I carried his official card from the Berlin Olympics in my wallet to keep my father with me. Then my wallet was stolen with the card, and my brothers and I were left only with this Amsterdam Olympic card.

Although my father liked to reminisce about water polo games he had played in Algiers or Barcelona, it did not occur to him to write about his career in sports. Once, in his beautiful handwriting, he began to recreate a history of his swimming career but, after a few pages, he stopped. I have completed what he began to celebrate his life and the lives of thousands of other Jewish sportsmen and sportswomen active in 20th century Central Europe.

Helen Epstein

June 2019

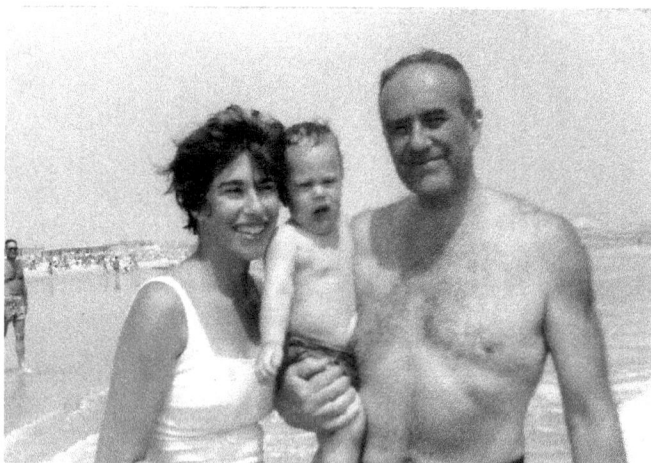

The author, her brother David and Kurt at the beach, c. 1962.

Although my mother was the custodian of memory in our family, my father — Kurt Epstein — is the one whose life is preserved in public documents: newspaper articles and photographs in the sports sections of Czechoslovak and other European newspapers, military and sports records. His ancestors were traditional Bohemian Jews, tanners by trade, who had lived in what is now the Czech Republic for four centuries. But rather than going to work in his father's leather business, Kurt Epstein became a champion swimmer and went on to play water polo in the infamous Nazi Olympics.

For nearly two decades, between 1918 and 1938, after organizing a group of schoolfriends to swim in the Elbe for fun, Epstein competed in hundreds of domestic races and represented Czechoslovakia in international water polo matches and two Olympic Games. Both before and after the Second World War, he was also a swim coach who served as a role model for younger generations of Czechoslovak men and women.

Maďarsko—Československo 4:3.

Čs. mužstvo, které čelilo ve vodním polu maďarským mistrům.

Kurt Epstein, 3rd from left.

The memory of Epstein's generation of European Jewish athletes is largely lost. Most of its members were murdered in the Holocaust and left few records. In addition, neither Nazi nor Communist policies encouraged preservation of Jewish history in the Czech lands. But Jewish scholarship, as sports sociologist George Eisen has pointed out, is also to blame.

Kurt and a teammate swimming in the Vltava.

"I cannot recall any subject in Jewish culture," he writes, "that could elicit such conflicting emotions, oscillating between a yawningly mild interest, bordering on apathy and an ardent apologia. In an almost collusive way, the scholarly community has vacillated between grudging recognition and a desultory dismissal of the idea of Jewish prominence in sports."

Kurt Epstein's life was, for the most part, typical of his generation of Czech and other Central European Jews. But that prototype has been subsumed both in Jewish and non-Jewish collective memory to several others. The more benign is the stereotype of the Prague Jewish intellectual Franz Kafka.

Franz Kakfa.

According to his friend Max Brod, Kafka was actually a health nut who hiked, sunbathed in the nude and swam in the Vltava whenever he could, but he has become in contemporary culture an icon of the solitary, neurotic, sexually inhibited Jew, far more at home indoors than outside. Like his contemporary in Vienna, Arthur Schnitzler, Kafka is perceived as a German-speaking coffeehouse Jew who devoted his time and energy to developing his mind rather than his body.

A less benign turn-of-the century stereotype common in anti-Semitic publications of the time is the avaricious indoor Jew.

Whether he keeps a small shop, is a player on the stock exchange, or works for a newspaper, this Jew is obsessed by the acquisition of money. He is flat-footed, pigeon-toed, narrow-shouldered and big-bellied, inhabiting what Sander Gilman has termed "the Jew's body."

The figure of the Jewish athlete does not easily lend itself to caricature. It flies in the face of both anti-Semitic stereotypes and Jewish humor, but it is becoming an important part of Jewish history.

Kurt as coach.

Kurt Epstein was born on January 29, 1904 in Roudnice-on-the-Elbe, a small Czech town at the foot of a solitary mound-like hill called the Říp. According to the Czech chronicler Cosmas of Prague in the early 12th century, the Říp was the place where the first Slavs, led by Forefather Čech, settled, giving his followers their name.

The Epstein family, according to a fragment of the chronicle my father began but did not finish, could be traced back to the fifteenth century. Roudnice was one of four major centers of Jewish settlement in the Czech lands and by the time Kurt was born, it was a town of about 12,000 people, 50 kilometers northwest of Prague, in the province of Bohemia in the Austro-Hungarian Empire.

The multi-ethnic Austro-Hungarian Empire.

Although he grew to be over six feet tall with the classic broad shoulders, long arms, and narrow hips of a swimmer, Kurt was a puny, premature baby and it was deemed too dangerous to perform a circumcision. Somehow, in the ensuing years, a mohel was never called to perform the ritual, and that fact as well as the precariousness of his first months may have helped predetermine Kurt's assimilationist identity.

The marriage of his parents, Helene Pollak and Maximillian Epstein, had been strictly traditional, arranged by a shadchan who matched two acculturated but solidly Jewish families. Helene's father was a grain merchant. Max had dropped out of school at the age of 10 to help his widowed mother Leopoldine run the family's tannery business but, by 1900, he was a pillar of Roudnice's Jewish community.

Roudnice, c. 1900.

Kurt's grandfather Jakob Epstein had been the first Jew in Roudnice granted permission to build a home outside the gated Jewish Street. In 1900,

Kurt's father Max had the original one-story house torn down, hired an architect, and replaced it with a two-story structure that included the then new-to-Roudnice amenities of indoor plumbing, electricity and a telephone. Now the premises of a regional museum, the building still has ornate capital Es for Epstein on the façade.

The Epstein house in Roudnice *(Sheila Pallay)*.

Later, Max would serve as head of the Jewish community and its Zionist group, conduct the synagogue choir and, in 1903, hire the young Richard Feder to serve as the community's rabbi. But now, at 28, he was ready for marriage.

Helena Pollak and Maximillian Epstein.

Helene Pollak was seven years younger than Max, born in 1879, one of fourteen Pollak children in the German-speaking tourist town of Reichenberg, now Liberec. German Jewish bourgeois families like the Pollaks could be in the avant-garde of social change in the Habsburg

Europe during the 1880s and 1890s, and Helene benefited from the various reform movements in dress, women's rights, education, physical culture and Judaism of the time. Although she arrived in Roudnice with no knowledge of Czech, she soon learned the language and, in her son's account, gave herself the name Helena, and became a fervent Czech patriot. She gave birth to Erich in 1902; Kurt in 1904; and Bruno in 1908.

Helena and her three sons.

Kurt did not often speak about either of his brothers but, when pressed, described Bruno as "childish" due to brain damage during a forceps delivery. It seems more likely that his younger brother was born what was then called "weak-minded," or now called "a person with mental impairment" in Czech — a source of shame and embarrassment that marked my father's life in many ways.

Bruno was regarded as the "village idiot." The most significant consequence of Bruno's retardation was that, in 1938, when Max obtained visas for his family to leave Czechoslovakia for Palestine, he was unable to obtain one for Bruno. Helena refused to leave without him; the rest of the family refused to leave without Helena; and as a result, all the Epsteins but for Kurt were deported and murdered by the Nazis.

"We were a well-to-do, assimilated family," Kurt said in an oral history taken in 1974. "When I was born, my father had a wholesale and retail business in leather for shoes and, in 1912, he built a factory for shoes for export. He exported shoes to England, Denmark, Yugoslavia, Romania, all over Europe." The Epstein boys played at being American cowboys; their parents employed a cook and a nurse, a German tutor and violin teacher. As a Zionist, Max taught his sons to deposit part of their spending money every week into the Keren HaKayemet box at the foot of the stairs. In the Austro-Hungarian Monarchy that preceded the Czechoslovak Republic of 1918, religious instruction in elementary school was obligatory three times a week, and Kurt studied Hebrew, the Jewish cycle of holidays and Jewish history with Rabbi Feder. Every year, the parents traveled to Carlsbad; every summer, the family vacationed on the Baltic Sea.

Helena, as she now was called, had turned 20 just before the turn of the century and, like many bourgeois girls of her generation rowed, and skated as well as swam. She undoubtedly heard about the first modern Olympic Games in Athens in 1896, where several Jewish participants had won medals.

She also followed the second Olympic Games in Paris, where 19 women competed in 1900. At a time of no radio, TV or many movies, the Olympics raised athletes — men and women — to the status of heroes. Whether or not Helena rode a bicycle or used a tennis racquet, she would have found neither exotic. It was his mother, not his father, whom Kurt Epstein credited with encouraging his interest in sports.

Scholars date the beginning of modern interest in organized sports to the Enlightenment and eighteenth-century fascination with the Greek ideal of the naked, athletic male body. Contemporary gymnastics began in post-Napoleonic Prussia where Friedrich Jahn, intent on strengthening the German military, started the German gymnastics organization, the Turnverein. The notion that athletic activity both strengthened individual character and national solidarity soon spread and European children were encouraged to take up hiking, swimming and gymnastics, a term which then included fencing, boxing and weight-lifting along with calisthenics. The Czechs were the first Slavs to start their own national gymnastics movement, the Sokol (Falcon) in 1862; others soon followed suit.

By 1910, when Kurt Epstein was six years old, training in gymnastics and participation in sports had become normative for all Czech children — girls and boys, Christians and Jews, children of factory workers as well as children of factory owners. For affluent Jews like the Epsteins, making sure that their sons knew how to swim, skate and row became part of self-cultivation and embourgeoisement. The Epsteins lived near the Elbe River and, early on, Kurt began to use it to skate, row, and swim.

Swimming, especially, provided fun, sensual pleasure and a form of therapy. "Any mood can be improved by a good swim," he would say for the rest of his life. But there's no question that from the start, Kurt also connected swimming with proof that Jews were as strong and athletic as everyone else. As an adult, he would often recall that he had organized a group of friends to swim, because anti-Semitic boys often threw stones. In 1990, when I visited Roudnice, a former neighbor confirmed his account: "We had a swim club when we were little. We met every week, each time at a different house so I knew your father's house very well. There were two brothers, two Jews and two Aryans. Well one of those was me."

Until the end of the First World War, what is now the Czech Republic was part of the Austro-Hungarian Empire and Max Epstein had been a loyal supporter of Emperor Franz Josef. Although he had been 42 years old in 1914, Max had fought for Austria-Hungary in the First World War in gratitude for the liberalizing policies that Franz Joseph had promulgated that had brought Jews freedom of movement and prosperity.

Max in uniform during World War I.

When the Austro-Hungarian Empire was defeated in 1918, and, as one of the consequences, Czechoslovakia became an independent nation,

Jews who had supported Austria were stigmatized. My father claimed that there had been no violence in Roudnice against Habsburg-identified Jews, but did remember that graffiti of gallows appeared on the walls of some Jewish businesses and the slogan "Nekupte u Epsteina; lepsi to ma starej Hajna!" (Don't buy at Epstein's; old Hajna's stuff is better!) was scrawled on the walls of their house.

In 1918, Kurt was 14 years old and, like most Czech teenagers, grew up in a climate of patriotic fervor, some of it instilled in school where nationalist Czech poetry was recited and Francophile songs sung. Even staunch monarchists like his father Max were compelled to admire the new president, Thomas Garrigue Masaryk. Jews throughout Europe spoke with awe and some envy of Czechoslovakia as a country whose president was a philosopher, concerned with the protection of the civil rights of minorities, and taught that anti-Semitism was long-debunked superstition. President Masaryk's circle included several prominent Jews and during the First Republic, intermarriage between Christians and Jews rose to 30% — on par with Berlin and Vienna.

Kurt at 14.

Kurt did not get involved in political conversations and found that sports was a place where he didn't have to. "I didn't want to be different from the rest of the population," he wrote. "I loved my mother very much but I resisted when she said 'you as a Jew have to behave twice as carefully as others in public.' I wanted to be like everyone else."

Unlike his father Max, who was already traveling on business at age 14, Kurt was being educated at Roudnice's Gymnasium, where he behaved like an entitled teenager. At 13, he had developed a crush on Boženka, the 12-year-old Catholic girl upstairs, carrying her books to school, and going for long walks with her after church on Sundays. Although this caused something of a small town scandal, neither set of parents intervened. When, during that time, Kurt overheard an anti-Semitic remark in a class where he was the only Jew, he packed up his schoolbag and walked out. He reported the incident to his parents who told his Rabbi, who complained to the school principal.

"At that time," Kurt recalled, "such an infraction of religious tolerance was not allowed. The teacher was reprimanded and I returned triumphantly three days later. From that time on, I was left in peace."

Čejka

Roku 1918: „Nám Čechům se nemůže nic stát."

Roku 1919: „Nám židům se nic nemůže stát."

Caricature of a Czech Jew, 1919.

That incident remained in his memory as emblematic both of Roudnice's and the new nation's legacy of anti-Semitism and of readily available recourse. Such persistent displays of anti-Semitic occurrences, he said later, was one of the reasons that he joined Roudnice's highly successful rowing club, which first introduced him to regular practice, athletic discipline, and objective measurements of accomplishment. His German teacher — a charismatic coach who over the course of his career, produced 80 competitive rowers — got him started. "I succumbed to the magic of this sport," Kurt wrote, "not only because it was good for my health but also because I tried to prove that Jews are physically just as capable as other people."

Rowing provided his first experience of competitive sports and the triumph of winning. It made him an asset to his school and sports-minded small town, and subsumed his Jewish identity. Kurt soon began to think about competitive swimming. His group that swam together in the Elbe followed newspaper reports of races in Prague and invested in a stopwatch to clock their own times. Since they were not much slower than the Prague swimmers, they enrolled in the next race. Kurt won in the 50-meter breast stroke. The group formed the Independent Swim Club of Roudnice, and Kurt decided to pursue competitive swimming.

His comfortable and doting parents encouraged him. Their eldest son, Erich, was studying at the German Business Academy in Prague, and they considered Kurt's excellence in sports as a talent to be cultivated. Sportsmanship was then viewed as a social asset to a middle class family. It would be a decade before the commercialization of sports would begin in earnest, with Olympic swimmer Johnny Weissmuller winning a contract to endorse

BVD swimwear, being cast as Tarzan and becoming a proponent, along with Lou Gehrig, of Wheaties, Breakfast of Champions.

Max and Helena, doting parents, 1918.

Kurt did not view sports as a way of earning his living. Very few sports at that time — boxing primarily — were regarded as careers. Rowing, fencing, running, and even soccer were for amateurs, lovers of the sport itself. Athletes expected to pursue their sport for the rest of their lives, alongside careers as physicians, lawyers, engineers, and businessmen. Advertisers were not yet capitalizing on the selling power of athletes.

According to scholar Claire Nolte, the Czech lands were home to the greatest density of sports clubs in Central Europe during the first decades of the Twentieth Century. Many thousands of Czechs attended Sokol, and thousands of Germans the Turnverein. The Turnverein, however, became increasingly anti-Semitic and in 1887, the Turnverein club of Vienna expelled the 400 Jews who constituted more than one third of its membership. Over the next decade, the majority of the Austrian clubs adopted what became known as the "Aryan paragraph" and barred Jews from membership. Although the Sokol was also strongly nationalistic and its leadership adopted anti-Catholic and anti-socialist exclusions in 1910, Sokol never adopted an "Aryan paragraph" although it did expel its Jewish members after the Nazi take-over.

In 1898, Dr. Max Nordau called for a "muscular Judaism" at the second Zionist Congress in Basel. Dr. Nordau, a physician and one of the visionaries of the Zionist movement, was adapting the idea of "Muscular Christianity," which had originated a few decades earlier in England. He argued that a muscular Jewry had existed in ancient times but over the centuries, had been destroyed.

Max Nordau.

"All the elements of Aristotelian physics — light, air, water, and earth — were measured out to us very sparingly," he said. "In the narrow Jewish street our poor limbs soon forgot their gay movements; in the dimness of sunless houses our eyes began to blink shyly; the fear of constant persecution turned our powerful voices into frightened whispers which rose in crescendo only when our martyrs on the stakes cried out their dying prayers in the face of their executioners. But now, all coercion has become a memory of the past, and at last we are allowed space enough for our bodies to live again. Let us take up our oldest traditions; let us once more become deep-chested, sturdy, sharp-eyed men... For no other people will gymnastics fulfill a more educational purpose than for us Jews. It shall straighten us in body and in character. It shall give us self-confidence..."

I don't know if my father read Nordau but he was well aware of the stereotype of the sickly Jew and eager to distance himself from it. Much of the Jewish community of Czechoslovakia was doing that at the time of the First Republic.

Sanitization of the ghetto, 1890s.

Prague's 400-year-old Jewish ghetto had been eradicated in a huge project of urban renewal that had begun in 1895 and was not entirely completed until the First World War. The asanace, or sanitizing, as it was called, had razed to the ground a squalid slum, replacing it with straight streets and modern buildings. It was a symbolic as well as a concrete act of destruction. In 1906, a Jewish Museum was founded, as if to relegate the old Jewish Town to the status of an historical exhibit.

At the beginning of the 20th century, Jews were by many measures, including lifespan, infant mortality, and rate of alcoholism, the healthiest group in Europe. Yet the Kafka stereotype persisted not only in German and Czech but in Jewish collective consciousness. Franz Kafka himself reportedly said, "In us all it still lives — the dark corners, the secret alleys, shuttered windows, squalid courtyards, rowdy pubs and sinister inns. We walk through the broad streets of the newly built town. But our steps and our glances are uncertain. Inside, we tremble just as before in the ancient streets of our misery. Our heart knows nothing of the slum clearance which has been achieved. The unhealthy old Jewish town within us is far more real than the new hygienic town around us."

When I asked my father in the 1970s why he had chosen to become a competitive swimmer, he replied as though it went without saying: "Swimming was the best sport for Jews because you didn't need physical power as much as willpower and endurance. Jews were not as physically developed as the gentiles because of what they inherited from a life in the ghetto."

Kurt as a young athlete.

After completing five years of Roudnice's Gymnasium, in 1920, Kurt was accepted at the Czech Business Academy in Prague-Karlin. "The change from a small town to a metropolis had a deep effect on me," he later wrote. "I realized I had to rely on myself alone." The four-year curriculum of 22 courses included shorthand and calligraphy, in which Kurt excelled. He became known for his beautiful handwriting and won an honorarium from the Savings Bank of Karlin to produce 900 members certificates by hand. But most of his memories of business school centered around the sports prowess of his teachers and fellow students: "Among the faculty was the famous rower and international secretary of the Olympic Committee Dr. Widrinsky. A well-known student was Jaroslav Drobný, the Davis Cup winner and outstanding hockey player."

During his last year of business school, Kurt was called up by his draft board. He recalled being processed "with a group of more or less under-developed young men and when my turn came, the draft commissar declared me 'fit without fault.'"

In the late 1960s and 1970s when American young men were resisting the military draft, Kurt would say "It never occurred to me to evade my responsibility as a citizen, to stay up all night and drink potfuls of coffee to produce an irregular heartbeat in order to be rejected."

Kurt took pride in joining the Czechoslovak Army in a way that mirrored his father's attitude toward serving Austria in the First World War.

Kurt (3rd from right) as reserve lieutenant in the Czechoslovak army, 1929.

In the fall of 1924, he was posted to Podolínec in Slovakia. "Podolínec was in Slovakia, near the Polish border — not even the train went any farther. Civilization had not reached it at that time. We washed in a brook and slept in a convent corridor," he wrote in his chronicle. Kurt was soon selected for reserve officers' school in Košice, where he underwent his three months of basic training.

Officer's school was, in Kurt's account, a haven for "sons of moneyed families" but the Košice Cadets Academy was hardly a spa: it had been built to house 350 men and there were 800 reservists.

Moreover, Kurt's commander, Major Tamasier, was a former member of the French Foreign Legion who had served in Africa and believed that an officer had to undergo 10 times as rigorous a basic training as an ordinary recruit. In addition to rising at 5 AM and learning to shoot, peel potatoes, wash floors, and march for twelve hours at a stretch, Kurt recalled that he learned two things that would later save his life: one was to stop being a picky eater; the second was to make split-second decisions. "We were taught that a wrong decision is better than no decision at all."

General Radola Gajda was Commander of the division and also demanded strict discipline from the officers-in-training. If Gajda encountered an officer in the city of Košice with his jacket lapel open, he would arrest him on the spot and punish him with 30 days of house arrest. When he first took over the division, a banquet was held in his honor. "In the middle of it, Gajda disappeared. He had gone to inspect the bakery, the laundry, and the warehouse; he found violations of protocol, meted out punishments, and returned to the banquet. I experienced his strictness myself and was not upset when he was replaced by General Šnejdárek."

Kurt credited basic military training in Košice with helping him survive the Nazi concentration camps.

In 1924, a network of Kurt's sports friends pulled strings to get him transferred to the cushy Officers' School for Administration in Dejvice-Prague, closer to his swim club ČPK, the Czechoslovak Swim Club.

It took two days to travel from Košice to Prague, where Kurt was given lodgings in a dormitory "with curtains, a well-stuffed mattress, and a nightstand." He wrote, "We were encouraged to decorate the walls and used cut-outs from *La Vie Parisienne* so that during inspections, the officer was more interested in details of the pictures than in the neatness of our beds."

In his account of officer's school, Kurt recalled learning about the importance of vitamins for the first time in a course about nutrition. But he often took advantage of the casual atmosphere by cutting classes to go swimming. Nonetheless he graduated and was posted to Litoměřice, where his duties were to supervise requisition and preparation of food for four kitchens feeding 300 soldiers and to keep the books.

He soon discovered that the books had been cooked. When Kurt received complimentary bottles of liquor and packages of cigarettes in what apparently were routine bribes, he told the providers to keep the pay-offs but to deliver exactly what they had been contracted to provide. The suppliers had friends in the Ministry of Defense and Kurt's office was subjected to an audit. Kurt was vindicated and developed a reputation as an honest officer that followed him through the war. That Christmas, when more than half of the garrison went on leave, the Jewish reserve lieutenant volunteered for duty supervising the preparation of Christmas dinner: fried carp with potato salad, tea with rum, and a small stollen.

In 1925, ČPK requested that he be furloughed for his first international water polo match, in Barcelona.

"At that time, people still traveled by train," he later recalled. "Our travel time to Barcelona was two days and two nights and we were there for a week. Our women swimmers caused a sensation because, back then, Spanish women were still not allowed to wear bathing suits in public. The water polo matches were a big social affair — men in tails, women in ballroom attire. The matches began at 10 in the evening and ended at midnight. We won most of them and we left very happily."

Spain was a deceptive introduction to the grueling matches that would follow with more belligerent national teams.

THE ROUGHEST GAME IN THE WORLD

ONE OF RUDDY'S FAVORITES- THE HAIR GRIP

JOE RUDDY USING AN ARM STRANGLE HOLD AND A LEG SCISSORS COMBINED, UNDER WATER

TWISTING A TOE TO BREAK A SCISSORS HOLD

THE LEG STRANGLE HOLD AS USED UNDER WATER

RUDDY HOLDING ONE MAN UNDER WITH AN ARM STRANGLE, AND ANOTHER OPPONENT HELPLESS WITH A JITSU TOE GRIP

THE KNEE GRIP

Copyright, 1920, by the Press Publishing Co.

A diagram of "the roughest game in the world".

Water polo developed in Scotland as aquatic rugby in the 1880s and soon spread to England, America and Central Europe. By the early 1920s it looked more like aquatic soccer, and was one of the most popular spectator sports — as well as one of the roughest. Matches were brutal. Referees could sometimes spot one swimmer holding an opponent's head under water but could only guess about what was going on out of sight: kicking of genitals and strangulation of limbs were the most prevalent tactics.

Water polo drew athletes unafraid of physical contact and one of Kurt's most often repeated water polo stories began: "We often played in Vienna. The progress of the match was broadcast to Prague and all of a sudden the broadcaster announced: 'The game is getting harder. Defense Epstein is now playing without his swim trunks.'"

It is tempting to ponder the psychology that drew men to such a rough sport. Kurt played water polo throughout Europe and North Africa, from Stockholm to Tangiers but felt that he learned the most from the Hungarian teams, who rarely lost a game. "In Budapest," he recalled, "we were once beaten 13-1. I asked their defense why he was playing so furiously since his team was already winning by two digits. He answered that after the First World War, each one of Hungary's neighbors had taken a piece of their land. Therefore it was important at least in sports to score as high as possible."

The Czechoslovak national water polo team. Kurt
is 2nd from right.

For my father, the ultimate place to score was at
the Berlin Olympics in 1936. He had played in 1928
in Amsterdam, when he was 24 years old.

In Berlin, he was 32, old for a swimmer but still
a contender in water polo. Whether or not to
participate in what would become known as the
Nazi Olympics was a hotly debated question
throughout the world. Campaigns to boycott Berlin
took root all over the world. A Gallup poll of 1935
indicated 43% of Americans favored boycott and
many American athletes refused to participate. The
international Maccabi sports union ordered all its

members to boycott, even though they faced expulsion from their national sports organizations if they did.

Kurt at the Brandenburg Gate, 1936.

In Czechoslovakia, there was a great deal of controversy among Jews about the propriety of participating in the Olympics of 1936. All the

Zionist sports clubs urged a boycott. Kurt was one of only two Jews who chose to compete for Czechoslovakia; and the only Jew on the seven-member water polo team who went to Berlin. Four others, including the country's best water polo player, Dr. Paul Steiner, joined the boycott.

Kurt felt that Jews were obliged to take part if only to refute the Nazi claim that they were inferior to the Aryans. When they crossed the border by train into Germany in August of 1936, Nazi flags hung from all the buildings and pictures of Hitler were to be seen in every shop window. Jewish doctors had already been barred from practicing medicine in German institutions.

And the previous month, the Sachsenhausen concentration camp had been established.

But inside the Olympic Village, there was almost no evidence of the Nazi regime. "We were about sixteen miles from the stadium," my father recalls. "Security was tight since the Nazis wanted to convey the impression of great order and authority. One hundred buses driven by soldiers were put at our disposal on a twenty-four hour basis. Every policeman we passed saluted us with a *Heil Hitler*, to which we invariably replied *At' žije Beneš* — Long live Beneš."

But, according to Kurt, the atmosphere in the Olympic Village was relaxed. Athletes exchanged stories and autographs in the barracks, at parties and in the dining hall. Only the Germans maintained an unnatural stiffness, coming to meals in closed ranks, taking seats on command and even marching in formation to the men's room, a practice that amused the rest of the Olympic community. Another novelty in 1936 was the appearance of a military parade through the village one night, when the Germans marched through bearing flags and old Teutonic standards.

But the most spectacular attraction at the Berlin Olympics was Hitler himself. My father had several opportunities to observe the Fuehrer. "He had a magical influence on the German athletes," he remembers. "In the javelin throw, for example, there were two Finns in the lead. Hitler appeared, the stadium gave him an ovation, and the next German contestant was so overwhelmed with emotion that he out-threw the Finns whom he had previously trailed badly."

Another day, Hitler went to watch a 1,500-meter race in which he hoped to encourage the German swimmers. By chance, my father had come to see the race and was sitting on the other side of the pool directly opposite him. During an intermission, a woman broke through the ring of guards and asked Hitler for an autograph. As he bent down to sign her book, she threw her arms around him and kissed him. The Fuehrer was so upset he turned red. He dismissed his bodyguards on the spot, left the stadium immediately and never returned. The incident was not reported. "I thought the woman was crazy," my father says. "She could have taken the opportunity to pull out a gun and shoot him. Unfortunately she didn't."

Kurt was one of the 3,963 athletes from 49 nations who played in the Nazi Olympics. Czechoslovakia did not win a medal for water polo. The Hungarians beat the Germans for the gold; the Germans won the silver; and the Belgians won the bronze.

Five Jews on Czechoslovak water polo team, 1936.
All but Kurt (2nd from right) boycotted Berlin.

When asked whether in retrospect he regretted his decision to participate, Kurt Epstein always answered no. He believed sports occupied a higher plane than politics and described the triumph of Jesse Owens, who defied Aryan notions of racial superiority by winning four gold medals.

"You could in no way harm the Nazis by withdrawing from the competition," he would say decades later. "I cheered when the American Negro Jesse Owens won four gold medals. It was an achievement that no Nazi race propaganda could deny."

Jesse Owens.

I know very little about my father's activities during the two years between those Olympics and the German Invasion of Czechoslovakia in March of 1939. But he often used the word "Munich" as a synonym for abject capitulation to bullying. The term "Munich" also came up when my parents entertained their refugee friends, and they argued for hours about the events that led up to the German invasion of Czechoslovakia in 1939 and the Second World War.

For them and all Czechs, Munich was personal. After annexing Austria, Hitler was determined to incorporate the Czech lands into Germany. His excuse was that about three million people who lived in Bohemia and Moravia were of German origin. For most of 1938 and 1939, Czechoslovak citizens who followed Hitler's rise assumed that Germany was preparing to invade Czechoslovakia. But their government had signed a military treaty with France, and a second one with the Soviet Union. In the event of a German invasion, they assumed that France and Great Britain would come to Czechoslovakia's defense. But France and Great Britain proved more interested in avoiding a military confrontation with Germany. In September of 1938, Hitler declared that he wanted the Czechoslovak army evacuated from the Sudetenland, where more than 50 per cent of the population was German. The Czechoslovak Army ordered a general mobilization and Kurt was called up.

"I heard the proclamation of mobilization by President Edvard Beneš at ten PM while I was playing billiards at a coffee house," Kurt later said in an interview. "I went home, changed into uniform and by midnight, I had reported to my commanding officer at Terezín."

The Czechoslovak Army, my father always said, was ready and well-prepared to fight the Germans. Then France and Great Britain capitulated to Hitler's demands. Kurt heard about it at his garrison. "When we heard that we had to demobilize, this was one of the saddest days of my life. Our commanding officer said good-bye, shaking every officer's hand as tears ran down his face. It was the first and last time I would see a colonel cry like a baby."

After his demobilization, Kurt recalled in an oral history, life in Prague changed very quickly. But he did not like to dwell on the past and his account of his life is spotty. In 1938, he was 34 years old and a champion swimmer, coaching water polo, working with his father, and representing leather factories in Czechoslovakia. Max, Helena and Bruno Epstein had moved from Roudnice to Prague in 1928. My father, who had a long-time girlfriend, was still maintaining the semblance of a residence with his parents in their large apartment.

The German army marched into Prague on March 15, 1939 and, six months later, started the Second World War by invading Poland.

As a Jew in Hitler's Protectorate, Kurt was subject to an increasing number of restrictions on where he could live and work, what he could own, where he could sit or walk and, of course, where he could swim. He never talked about the loss of his civil rights or about being obliged to wear a yellow star or about how he learned, in the summer of 1941, that Jews were being forcibly deported from Prague.

Kurt was himself deported on December 1 to the Terezín garrison where he had been a reserve lieutenant. He was one of a group of one thousand Jewish men whose forced labor was to transform it into Ghetto Theresienstadt. "When we arrived, there was nothing there," Kurt later recalled. "They put us in large rooms that had been used for dry goods and uniforms. We slept on concrete floors. There was no wood, not even a blade of straw. And the temperature was freezing. It was winter."

At first, Kurt, worked alongside the other men building structures to house incoming transports of prisoners. Then, when it was realized that he had been a quartermaster for the Czechoslovak army in this very place, he was made one of eight quartermasters — most of them former Army reserve officers like himself — charged with the feeding of thousands of prisoners.

He and the others rose at four or five in the morning to supervise the delivery of meat that was clearly stamped "not for human beings," and then its distribution, along with potatoes and other foodstuffs to the kitchens. "And of course there were good and bad people in Terezín and you couldn't always prevent stealing, but I tried to make sure that the products that were to be used for meals actually made it into the soup — for example, the margarine. Often, the cooks stole margarine for themselves to eat or to sell, so I tried to prevent this.

"And I had to keep daily records of what I received and what I used. I did this for almost three years and since I was not married, I was able to protect my parents and keep them with me in Terezín. They were shipped to Auschwitz in May of 1944 and it was a most difficult time of my life. I had to decide whether to go with them or stay behind. Friends told me to remain in Terezín — that the old people went to some other place and I would only be with them for the transport, we would be separated later. We didn't know what was happening in Auschwitz but we knew it wasn't good."

The following October, Kurt and his friends were deported to Auschwitz where they remained for only 48 hours. "There I had a very unusual experience," Kurt recalled in his oral history. "We went out of the trains and I was marching toward Dr. Mengele who was making a selection. When I stood before him, he asked me if I was healthy and I answered, without thinking. 'Yes I am.' But I had just been sick and I looked in bad shape, especially since I had not shaved in three days. I said, 'Yes.' So I passed the first test."

After 20 minutes, the men were selected for forced labor and ordered to form three lines. Most of Kurt's friends formed the first one and he joined them. But then — in what he later said was a matter of a fraction of a second — he changed his mind. That line was subsequently sent to work in a mine and no one survived. A second line formed and no one in it survived either. But of the third line, which Kurt joined with two friends, a businessman Pepik Aleš, and the Czech conductor Karel Ančerl, 96 men managed to survive the forced labor camp to which they were sent.

After the war and for the rest of his life Kurt would wonder whether it was God, a sixth sense, or pure luck that he had chosen to step out of the first group and stand with the third group. That group was first sent to a stone quarry an then to a propeller factory, not far from the Czechoslovak border. "We worked 12-hour shifts, one week during the day and one week at night. We had to walk about three miles a day and we were fed only 700 calories per day." Kurt credited his friendships with helping him survive the inhuman conditions. When one of the three friends was in a bad mood, the other two cheered him up. Kurt gave Ančerl lectures about water polo and the Olympics; Ančerl taught Kurt about conducting orchestras.

They were liberated in Friedland-Silesia by Russian officers on horseback, equipped with rifles, who told them they were free to return to Czechoslovakia. "They didn't seem to care too much about us. So we went to the nearest town, got rid of our prison uniforms and got some bread and, because we were tired, went to sleep — after so many years — in a fresh bedroom equipped with linens and pillow and had a good sleep. The next day we walked about 15 miles on foot towards the border."

When Kurt returned to Prague after the war, he had lost about 70 pounds, had dangerously low blood pressure, and a bad abscess on his foot. He was also very depressed. His parents and both his brothers had been gassed in Auschwitz.

His friend Pepik Aleš had a non-Jewish wife who had managed to save much of his business. For a time, Kurt lived with them, then found his own apartment. He returned to swimming and coaching, reconnected with his teammates and was elected to the Czechoslovak Olympic Committee. Then one day, on the street he met a Franci Solar, a young widow and dress designer whom he remembered coaching when she was a teenager. They moved in together after two days and were married at the end of 1946. I was born in November of 1947.

Kurt and Franci at Prague City Hall, 1946.

Kurt went back to Roudnice only once after his return to Czechoslovakia and before emigrating to America. Strangers were living in his house. The centuries-old Jewish community no longer existed. He hired a lawyer to handle all matters concerning his family's property and never returned again.

Kurt and Franci Epstein bought an apartment at the foot of Wenceslas Square above the Koruna restaurant, where my mother also established a fashion salon. He was working for his friend Pepik

Aleš and coaching the national water polo team when, in February of 1948, the Communists took over the country.

In 1938, Kurt had felt that, as a Czechoslovak citizen, reserve officer, and nationally-acclaimed athlete, he owed it to his country to remain. But in 1948, even though he was then 44 years old and didn't speak any language but Czech, he said, "I didn't want to make the same mistake like I did under the Nazis. After that experience, the three things that were most important to me were first — freedom; second — health; and third — contentment. The main reason I wanted to leave was for the sake of my child. I wanted that my child will live in a free country without any experience what I had to suffer."

Just after the Communist take-over, Kurt accompanied the national water polo team to France and from there, telegraphed his relatives — a favorite cousin had married Walter Petschek — in New York City to ask for help in arranging emigration. My mother was reluctant to leave Prague and worried about how they would make a living in America, but did not argue with my father.

Kurt and Franci's immigration papers.

We arrived in New York City in the summer of 1948 where, for a decade, Kurt was unable to find steady employment but where he was soon elected Treasurer of an expatriate organization called The Association of Czechoslovak Sportsmen in Exile in the Western World. Eventually, he was accepted into the ILGWU and became a cutter in a clothing factory in New York's garment district.

His wartime friend Pepik Aleš also emigrated to New York; Karel Ančerl eventually became the conductor of the Toronto Symphony Orchestra. And for the rest of his life, Kurt maintained a weekly correspondence with his best friend and former goalie of ČPK's water polo team, Engineer Josef Bušek, a Czech Christian who had remained in Prague. In fact, he corresponded with a network of Czech athletes-in-exile — Jewish and non-Jewish

Kurt as a cutter in New York's garment district.

— living in Australia, South America, Israel and Europe. He read the sports section of the newspaper every day, following swimming, tennis and ice hockey, and never lost his belief in the international brotherhood of sports and his right to define his own place in it.

He also kept in close touch with the survivors of the Jewish community of Roudnice and with his childhood Rabbi Dr. Richard Feder (1875-1970), sending them all money when he could.

Dr. Feder, whose wife and children were murdered in the war, had become a national icon in Czechoslovakia after the Holocaust. In 1959, he wrote this to my father in America:

"We suffered a great deal and there are so few of us left that we get completely lost in a crowd and have become quite insignificant. Even today, many of us are dying from the consequences of our suffering. We've become reserved and have almost stopped going to coffeehouses. In former times, people would say that the Jew was created for the coffeehouse; today that's no longer true. I'd like to know if in New York Czech Jews somehow get together and if they stick together to some degree and are closer to one another."

Dr. Richard Feder.

I don't know what my father replied to his old rabbi. In fact, his New York social set was not too different from the one he had enjoyed in Prague. It was comprised almost entirely of Czech refugees with a few athletic Viennese and Hungarians thrown in for seasoning. Some were Jewish; some were not. All were refugees from either Nazism or Communism. They saw one another often — not in coffeehouses, but on ski slopes, in state parks, at the

Central Park ice skating rink, at concerts, and in one another's homes, where they ate rich Central European pastries and argued loudly over history and politics in a way that would have been impossible in Prague.

Although Kurt Epstein never expressed any doubt about his decision to become an American, Czech remained his primary language and he never gave up his identity as a Czech Jew. In his will, he specified that, in addition to the customary Jewish service, the Czech national anthem be played at his funeral. It was, and Kurt Epstein's obituaries — in Czech and in English language papers — noted that he was a Czechoslovak athlete, the only person in his immediate family to survive the Second World War, and a Jew who had participated in the Nazi Olympics.

Kurt Epstein (1904-1975).

Acknowledgments

I would like to thank my brothers Tom Epstein (named after Thomas G. Masaryk) and David Epstein for their help in preparing this manuscript, Susan Hecker Ray for proof-reading, and Elisabeth Benjamin for assisting with the accompanying photographs.

I am indebted to my patient, persevering and always meticulous husband Patrick Mehr for bringing this book into the world.

ALSO BY HELEN EPSTEIN

Archivist on a Bicycle: Jiří Fiedler

Children of the Holocaust

Joe Papp: An American Life

Looking Back: Memoir of a Psychoanalyst
(with Paul Ornstein)

Meyer Schapiro: Portrait of an Art Historian

Music Talks: the lives of classical musicians

The Long Half-Lives of Love and Trauma

Tina Packer Builds A Theater

Where She Came From: A Daughter's Search for
Her Mother's History

Writing from Life

Plunkett Lake Press eBooks

Lucie Aubrac
Outwitting the Gestapo

Lucy S. Dawidowicz
From That Place and Time: A Memoir, 1938-1947

Inge Deutschkron
Outcast: A Jewish Girl in Wartime Berlin

Charles Fenyvesi
When The World Was Whole

Sebastian Haffner
Defying Hitler: A Memoir
The Meaning of Hitler

Eva Hoffman
Lost in Translation

Kathryn Hulme
The Wild Place

Egon Erwin Kisch
Sensation Fair: Tales of Prague

Heda Margolius Kovály
Under A Cruel Star: A Life in Prague, 1941-1968

For more information, visit plunkettlakepress.com

www.ingramcontent.com/pod-product-compliance
Lightning Source LLC
Chambersburg PA
CBHW021212020426
42331CB00003B/320